Overcoming the

Battles of Life

Overcoming the

Battles of Life

Blondell Thomas

© Copyright December 2018 Blondell Thomas

All rights reserved. This book is protected under the copyright laws of the United States of America. No portion of this book may be reproduced in any form, without the written permission of the publisher. Permission granted on request.

Published by: Unlock Publishing House, Maximized Productions
6715 Suitland Road
Morningside, Maryland 20746
www.unlockpublishinghouse.com
ISBN: 978-1732750333

Cover Design by Maximized Productions – Graphics Division of UPH, Inc.
Unless otherwise indicated, Bible quotations are taken from:

New King James Version (NKJV): Scripture taken from the New King James Version®. Copyright © 1982 by Thomas Nelson. Used by permission. All rights reserved.

New International Version (NIV): Holy Bible, New International Version®, NIV® Copyright ©1973, 1978, 1984, 2011 by Biblica, Inc.® Used by permission. All rights reserved worldwide.

Living Bible (TLB): The Living Bible copyright © 1971 by Tyndale House Foundation. Used by permission of Tyndale House Publishers Inc., Carol Stream, Illinois 60188. All rights reserved.
Amplified Bible (AMP) Copyright © 2015 by The Lockman Foundation, La Habra, CA 90631. All rights reserved.

Amplified Bible (AMPC): Amplified Classic Edition Copyright 1954, 1958, 1962, 1964, 1965, 1987 by The Lockman Foundation

Printed in the United States of America Deceember2018

DEDICATION PAGE

Thank you Jesus, who always comes first in my life. I know without your grace and mercy, I wouldn't be here today. You have spared my life, and I thank you.

To my beloved husband, the late James Thomas, for his loving and loyal support over the 32 years of our marriage. I thank God for sending you into my life to give me hope when I had lost hope, and for giving me a desire to live again. I will always love you.

To my two sons, Victor Bradford and Everette Bradford, my two daughters, Annette Thompson, and Rakima Stokes Little, I love you guys so very much. To my daughter-in-law, Zena Bradford and Latasha Bradford, my son-in-law, Kenneth Thompson, and Johnathan Little, thank you guys for enriching our family, I love you guys. To all of my grandchildren and great-grandchildren, I love you, and you will always have a special place in my heart.

Finally, to my mother, the late Sarah Hawkins Graves, a mighty woman of God who taught me how to live by the principles of God, I am so privileged to have been raised by a mother like you.

TABLE OF CONTENTS

CHAPTER 1 ~ SEEKING FOR LOVE --------------------- 13

CHAPTER 2 ~ BEING ANXIOUS ------------------------ 18

CHAPTER 3 ~ VERY PRESENT HELP IN THE TIME OF TROUBLE -- 25

CHAPTER 4 ~ GOING THROUGH THE PAIN ----------- 30

CHAPTER 5 ~ LETTING GO OF THOSE THINGS THAT ARE BEHIND YOU -- 33

CHAPTER 6 ~ HAVING A FORGIVING SPIRIT --------- 38

CHAPTER 7 ~ THE WEAPON OF PRAYER ------------- 42

CHAPTER 8 ~ DYING TO SELF -------------------------- 50

CHAPTER 9 ~ CASTING YOUR CARES UPON HIM --- 54

CHAPTER 10 ~ MAINTAINING YOUR PEACE --------- 58

CHAPTER 11 ~ FIGHTING THE FIGHT OF FAITH --- 62

CHAPTER 12 ~ PREPARED FOR BATTLE ------------- 66

CHAPTER 13 ~ FIGHTING FOR MY SON -------------- 69

CHAPTER 14 ~ A LASTING ENCOUNTER -------------- 75

CHAPTER 15 ~ HEALING AND RESTORATION ------- 78

CHAPTER 16 ~ KNOWING YOUR WEAPONS --------- 82

CHAPTER 17 ~ STRENGTH AND POWER ------------- 89

ACKNOWLEDGMENTS

I acknowledge you Jesus, for moving on my spirit to write this book. I know without your grace and mercy, I wouldn't be here today.

To Annette, Victor, Everette, Rakima, thank you for loving and supporting me. I thank God for you guys every day.

Monica Thompson, thank you for encouraging me to tell my story.

To Pastor Ruth Hart, thank you for your prayers and inspiration.

To Ann Addison, thank you for your prayers and for being a faithful friend.

To Sharyn Jordan, thank you for giving me encouragement beyond what you can imagine.

I would like to thank Apostle Michael Goings of Outreach Family Fellowship for always being there for me.

And thank you to Apostle Michael Freeman and Dr. DeeDee Freeman of Spirit of Faith Christian Center, you have taught me so much and have been such an inspiration to me.

x

INTRODUCTION

This book will shed light on many truths, some that you may already know. Be sensitive to the Holy Spirit as He leads and guides you into all truth. This book is designed to help you deal with the issues of life and show you how to overcome God's way. It will show you how to connect God's truth with the situation you are facing now.

The battle against darkness is not diminishing. We are entering what the Bible calls the fullness of time, and there is so much at stake. God is positioning us, as believers to overcome these battles in order to advance His Kingdom, understanding that we have been set free in order to free others. But we can't free others if we haven't been set free, so we must ensure that we are equipped to do so.

Chapter 1
Seeking for Love

Matthew 6:33 "Seek first the kingdom of God, and His righteousness, and all these things shall be added unto you."

On a misty, rainy day in November 1978, as I waited to board the bus, I had a queasy feeling within my stomach that something terrible was going to happen.

Two weeks before had really been a very tough time for my three children and me, and even now everything was still very much unsettled. As I boarded the bus, my thoughts shifted back to the events leading up to this day.

My first husband, who was abusive (mentally and physically), had abused me for the last time. I had decided to move out of the house with the children. To make this transition, I located an apartment, made a deposit, and was prepared to move in within the next two weeks. A sigh of relief engulfed my body as I thought of leaving this life behind and making a better life for my children. I knew I had to keep this move to myself until the apartment was available. It was a perfect small two-bedroom apartment. The thought of freedom caused me to become excited.

To digress for a moment. I grew up in the South in a large family of twelve children. My father left home, leaving my mother with the responsibility of raising twelve children alone. I never really knew my father. The first time I remembered seeing him, I was a teenager. When my younger sister and I were introduced to him, he did not know me from my sister. This encounter left a long-lasting feeling of not being loved by my father, which has stayed with me even until today.

My mother was a strong Christian woman who did all she could to make up for us not having a father in our lives. She taught us strong principles and values. She taught us how to trust God, and I have passed these same principles and values on to my children.

I have always desired to have the love of my father, even with all the love my mother provided. I still was left with a sense something was missing i.e., there was a void and emptiness in my life. Thus, I grew up looking for that one person who could really love me and fulfill that void I had inside of me. Little did I know at the time, God was the only one who would be able to fill that void in my life. With that revelation I knew no matter what I would try to do, I would always be left with that emptiness inside of me unless I had God. You see, we were all created with that void in our hearts so it may draw us to God. He is the only one we truly need, and He is the only one who knows exactly how to supply that need.

I knew God at an early age. I knew right from wrong, but I was never taught the Word of God to the understanding I have now. Not fully understanding the true meaning and price of disobedience, I chose to disobey God by looking for love in all the wrong places.

At the age of 17, I became pregnant. I realized that I had disappointed my mother and was afraid to tell her about my situation. Being young and inexperienced, I kept my pregnancy a secret as long as I could. As the months passed,

I noticed my stomach expanding and realized I could not keep this secret much longer. I wore loose-fitting clothing and shift dresses, which were popular in that era. I stayed out of my mother's presence as much as possible.

I was a junior in high school, and I continued to attend school, living my life as normal as possible. One day at school, my Home Economics Teacher called me into her room to talk with me in private. The first thing she asked me was, "Are you pregnant?" I tried to deny it at first, but I realized I needed to talk to someone about my situation. I was so burdened with the pressure of trying to keep my pregnancy a secret for so long, that I begin to cry and admitted the truth to her. My teacher, who was very fond of me, recommended helping me to terminate the pregnancy. I knew she loved me and was concerned about me finishing school, but the thought of an abortion was inconceivable to me.

I wanted my unborn child and had already begun to love and bond with this life that was now growing inside of me. My teacher strongly recommended that I tell my mother, which I did. I will never forget, even to this day, the hurt and disappointment I saw on my mother's face when I broke the news to her. She sat quietly for a few minutes without replying, as she rocked back and forth in a chair on our front porch.

Finally, she looked up at me and said, "Blondell, I knew you were pregnant, but I was in denial. I just didn't want to accept it." But she said, "I also know God doesn't make mistakes and He will provide." Oh, what a relief! "This part is over," I said to myself, as I hugged my mother and we both cried.

Through this experience, Jesus began to show me there was a greater and higher purpose for me to seek from Him, for the fulfilling of my needs. He showed me the only way God's blessings would be released into my life was to seek God's way of doing things. Then I would receive answers to the problems I was confronted with and would have God's supernatural intervention in my life. Jesus showed me that if I would do it God's way, all of my needs would become His righteousness. Then all these things I needed would be added unto me.

Jesus began to tell me that He knew what I liked and He knew the things I craved. He also showed me nothing I bought for myself, nothing I put on or nothing I parked in my driveway had fulfilled me, because He was what I really needed. He told me He was the only one who could satisfy my thirst and when I became satisfied with Him, there were things I would never need again.

As I begin to read and meditate on God's Word, I came to the understanding that when we receive Christ in our lives by faith, we receive His righteousness. *II Peter 1:4* tells us that we are partakers of His divine nature and have the ability to live our lives as He lived His life, in complete victory over sin. The choice is ours to obey or disobey God. No one can make us disobey Him; once we have received Him, we have power over our actions.

Romans 6:12 – 16, tells us not to let sin reign in our mortal bodies, for sin shall not have dominion over us: For whom we yield ourselves servants to obey, we are servants to whom we obey. We can choose to obey God and live in victory, enjoying His blessings and have eternal life or we can disobey Him and live a defeated life. Again, the choice is ours.

Chapter 2
Being Anxious

Philippians 4:6 "Be anxious for nothing; but in everything by prayer and supplication with thanksgiving let your request be made known unto God."

My boyfriend was a senior in high school at the time. He decided he would finish school, get a job and we would get married. A few months later, I found myself standing before the Justice of the Peace quoting marriage vows which really had no meaning to me.

Shortly after we were married, my husband moved to Washington, DC with the hope of finding a better job and making a better life for his family. I followed about a year later with our two small children, ages 3 and 4. The city was new to me having been raised in the South. I had no immediate family there and was solely dependent upon my husband for everything.

The marriage started out all right for the first few years. However, as time went on, my husband became more and more abusive. After my youngest son was born, I went back to school to obtain my diploma and continued on to business school. After I finished business school, I found a job working for the federal government.

I was so overjoyed and happy to begin my career and earn money to help support my family; but unfortunately, that joyfulness was not shared by my husband. I began to notice how jealous he was becoming. He did not want me to buy anything for myself or get my hair done. When I did go shopping, my daughter would have to sneak the things in the house for me. On one occasion when I returned home from the beauty salon, he poured a bucket of water over my new hairdo. If I was late arriving home from work, there would be an argument that would many times escalate into a physical fight.

At some point, my husband began to stay away from home for days at a time, without calling to check on the children and me. Sometimes this went on for many days as well as nights; I found myself home alone with my three children.

When he would decide to return home, I would try to talk to him and asked him what was I doing wrong? He would say to me "It's not you…, It's me". If I would ask him where he had been, he would reply, "at my friend's house." I knew by his tone of voice not to press any further.

I was so hurt and confused because I really loved my husband and wanted him to love me. There were nights that I would cry myself to sleep feeling so alone and dreading facing another day. I thought the only thing that was keeping me going was the love for my children, not realizing at the time that it was God's grace that was undergirding me.

I kept on trusting God and asking Him to make me strong. Somehow, I knew He was always there with me, strengthening and upholding me. He has never left me or forsaken me but at that time in my life, I didn't know Jesus as well as I know Him now and I felt so all alone.

I remained in that marriage for 16 ½ years, abused and misused, hoping for a change that never came. I stayed in that abusive relationship because I wanted my children to be raised by both of their parents. I did not want them to go through what I went through by not having the love or support of a father. Little did I realized at the time what they were experiencing was far worse.

One day as I was sitting alone feeling sorry for myself, I began to talk to the Lord. I told the Lord I just couldn't take the abuse anymore. All the years of arguing and fighting had really taken a toll on me, and it was also affecting my children. It was then that I decided I was the one that had to take full responsibility for my children and do something about our current situation.

I found an apartment for my children and me and was preparing to move within the next two weeks; i.e., the apartment would not be ready for two weeks. I had paid down on some used furniture and made arrangements for the date of delivery. I knew I had to keep all of my preparations a secret for fear of what my husband may do to me if he found out. I was so afraid.

One Friday afternoon, I went to make the final payment on the apartment and sign the contract. On the way back home, I stopped to buy a treat for the children and me. As I returned home, I was surprised to see my husband's car in the driveway. Fear gripped my heart. I began to perspire, and my heart was beating so fast that it actually felt like it was skipping beats. Even though he was seldom at home, he did not allow me to go out unless I was going to work. He would sometimes take me to work himself. As I walked in the door, he begins slapping me around and making accusations. I tried to explain to him and show him what I had bought, but he wouldn't listen. He just continued to make all kinds of accusations. He snatched my purse from my shoulders and found the signed contract for the apartment I was going to rent and tore it into pieces.

A fight broke out so fierce that the children were crying and afraid. I could not comfort them because I was afraid for my life. After it was over, I was unable to use my left arm and feared it may have been sprained. The next morning before leaving for work, he threatened me and made a promise that he would kill me if I would ever try to leave him. So I took out a restraining order because he had threatened me and I was really afraid. I called my sister who lived in New Jersey and explained to her what had happened the previous night, and I told her I was afraid. She advised me to leave and come to New Jersey (where she lived) until my apartment became available.

I tried to explain to her that I just couldn't pull my children out of school in the middle of the school year. She advised me that for my safety, I should leave the children because he wouldn't hurt them but he might hurt me or worse.

I had never been separated from my children. This was one of the hardest decisions I ever had to make. Although my daughter was 16 years old at the time and was capable of taking care of her younger brothers, it did not change the fact it was one of the hardest decisions I ever had to make. I took my sister's advice, and she wired me the money while my husband was at work. With tears in my eyes, I hugged my children and said goodbye. I told them I would be back for them within a week and told my daughter to take care of her brothers.

I boarded the Amtrak that afternoon and traveled to New Jersey, crying all the way there. I wore dark sunglasses so no one would be able to see that I was crying. Monday morning, I called my job and told my supervisor I had a family emergency and needed a leave of absence for a week. My sister took me to see her doctor to have my arm examined. It turned out to be a pulled muscle. Praise God!

When it was time for me to leave, my three sisters who lived in New Jersey, pleaded with me not to return to Maryland. They told me they feared something terrible would happen. I assured them my apartment would be ready within the next week and I would be all right. They made me promise I would be careful and to call them as soon as I got settled in my apartment. The next Sunday I returned home to Maryland and went by the house to check on the children after making sure that my husband was at work. I explained to them that we would be moving into our apartment on that Tuesday. They were so happy to see me after being gone from them for a week, and I was so happy to see them as well.

When I called to check on the children before going to work the next morning, my daughter told me her father found out I was back in Maryland. She told me he had put all of them in the car and drove around until late that Sunday night looking for me. She also told me he was acting crazy and asking her all kind of questions about where I was staying, and she felt I shouldn't go to work. I assured her that I would be all right.

I did not have my car which left me having to catch the bus to work that Monday morning. As the bus was nearing my stop, my focus shifted back to today. Why do I have this eerie feeling?? Oh well, I thought, everything is going to be all right. I realize as I think back now, that God was trying to warn me of danger. If only I would have taken the time to listen to my spirit.

I began working right away because my desk was piled up from being off work for a week. While I was pre-occupied with my work, I heard one of my co-workers call my name. As I looked up, my husband was standing in front of my desk. He said, "I want to talk to you." I was so afraid but didn't want to make a scene, so I went out in the hallway to talk with him. He asked me to come back home, and I told him I wasn't coming back. I told him I was too tired to take any more abuse and it was just too much for the children. I asked him to please leave because I had to get back to work. He asked me to ride down with him on the elevator, and he would leave. So, we rode down, and he rode back up, we rode down, and again he rode back up, promising to leave. Little did I know at the time, he was trying to get me alone in the elevator, but each time we went up and down on the elevator, someone else would always be on the elevator.

Finally, I told him for the last time I had to get back to work. I remember him asking me if it was my final decision not to come back, and I replied "Yes." I told him I refused to come back to that marriage and be subjected to more abuse. The next thing I remembered I was laying by the elevator bleeding profusely. I guess I must have been in shock because I couldn't scream or say a word, as he continued stabbing me. Plus, I was ashamed that everyone would know I had been abused. I know that sounds crazy and messed up, but at the time, that was how I felt. I had tried to lie and cover up the truth for so long, and now the truth would come out. For some strange reason, I always was too embarrassed for anyone to know I was living in an abusive relationship.

I remember lying to my co-workers once about a black eye he had given me. The story was my husband was hanging panel and slipped and accidentally hit me in the eye. I don't know if they really believed me, but these were the type of stories I would tell when I had unexplainable bruises.

I would like to stop here and advise anyone who may be in an abusive relationship to get out and get some help. These types of relationships generally do not change. You are hoping for a change that will not come unless you get some counseling or get "Jesus" in both of your lives.

I must have thrown up my hands in defense because most of the damage was done to my hands. As I lay there, I can remember praying "Lord, I don't want to die." What would happen to my children? Then I remembered hearing in the distance the sound of the mail cart. The mail was being delivered to the various offices. Looking back now, I realize it must have been the mail cart distracting him, causing him to stop stabbing me. More importantly, I know it is only by the grace of God I am alive today writing this story.

Chapter 3
A Very Present Help in the Time of Trouble

Psalms 46:1 "God is our refuge and strength, a very present help in trouble."

A voice within me said, "Run." Somehow, by the grace of God, I got up and began to run and scream "somebody help me!!!" I ran into the office where I worked and heard someone say, "oh my God," it's Blondell! By this time, I was a bloody mess, and I remembered my supervisor grabbing me to stop me from running while asking someone to bring some pillows. My co-workers began to surround me and one of them whom I had previously carpooled with asked where the children were? I replied that they were in school and then everything became blurry and confused. I could hear voices which seemed somewhat distant.

Someone had called for help, and there were doctors and nurses over me applying pressure to stop the bleeding. My husband had stabbed me 13 times. I was rushed to the hospital with a punctured lung with nerves and tendons cut in both hands where I had tried to defend myself. In the building where I worked the doctor's office was located on the fourth floor, and I worked on the sixth floor. As the doctor and nurses were working on me, I remembered asking them how they had gotten there so fast. (I knew the elevators in my opinion, were very slow.) The nurse smiled at me and said whenever we have an emergency; we don't take the elevators, we take the stairs.

The ambulance arrived, and I was rushed to the closest hospital. For those of you who have never ridden in an ambulance (my prayer is that you will never have to.) I would like to inform you that is one of the most uncomfortable rides you probably will ever take. I was thrown from side to side as the bed I was laying on was sliding all over the place. When I arrived at the hospital, approximately twelve doctors and nurses begin working on me to stop the bleeding. I was given so many shots until I felt like a pen cushion. I was unable to breathe on my own because one of my lungs was punctured. I was given an oxygen mask to help me breathe. I felt so helpless being at the mercy of the doctors and nurses.

As they continued to work on me, I caught the eye of one of the nurses who would later come to visit and encourage me every day. God always has someone there for you no matter what you may be going through. He is faithful to His Word, that He will never leave you or forsake you. This nurse later shared with me when they brought me in and when she first looked at me, she knew something was different about me. I told her I was a Christian and she replied that she was able to tell. Praise God! God gave me favor with all of the nurses and the doctors. They all knew my name and would always have something encouraging to say. After all, I had stayed in the hospital for about two months. I would see them almost every day so they became like a second family to me.

Those days I spent in the hospital were not pleasant ones. Sometimes I would be in so much pain that I was unable to stay in bed. All I could do was cry out to God for relief as I walked the floor. I can tell you that somehow I knew God was always there with me and He kept His promise that He would never leave me or forsake me. As I think back on those days in the hospital, it sometimes brings tears to my eyes when I see how far God has brought me. I would lay there in that hospital bed day after day feeling lonely, with both of my hands elevated and wrapped in bandages. I felt as helpless as a small child unable to feed myself or bathe myself. I was unable to go to the bathroom by myself or clean myself. All sense of dignity was taken away from me.

Regardless of what anyone may say, no one can feed you like you want to be fed. They will either feed you too slowly or they will feed you too fast. There was no room for me to be embarrassed when I had to be taken to the bathroom and the nurse would have to clean me because I was unable to do it myself. I would find myself holding on as long as I could because I didn't want to call for the nurse to take me to the bathroom. I was always at the mercy of others, but God always extended His hand of mercy toward me, and that is what I was able to hold on to, and that is what brought me through this battle.

I stayed in intensive care for two weeks because I was so weak from losing so much blood. I was finally moved to a room and was so happy at the thought of being able to see my children again! I actually thought I was going home, but I was in for a great disappointment. I shared my excitement with my favorite nurse, and the expression on her face changed from gladness to sadness. I asked her what was wrong and she explained to me that I wouldn't be going home right away and at that moment all my joy turned to sadness.

Later the doctor came in and explained to me that I would have to have surgery on both of my hands. He told me they were unable to do the surgery in the beginning because I was too weak from losing so much blood and they had to build my strength up first. He proceeded to tell me that he believed in being honest with his patient. He continued to tell me the surgery would take about eight hours. He explained that I had a lot of damage done to both of my hands. He explained to me that the nerves were cut in my right hand, and the nerve and tendons were cut in my left hand. He then said, "You will not be able to use your left hand and will only have little or no use of your right hand. At that moment, I felt like I was having a bad dream as a rush of emotions came over me. I began to cry. The doctor just looked at me and walked out of the room.

I wondered how could the doctor just come in and tell me news like that and then walk away. He didn't even try to comfort me. Doesn't he realize I don't have any family here to talk to or to comfort me? "Oh God," I said. What am I going to do? I don't want to live if I can't use my hands! At that moment, one of the mothers of the church I attended walked in and asked me what was wrong. I told her what the doctor had just told me. She looked at me and said, "Stop crying." Don't you know there's a doctor above all doctors and His name is Dr. Jesus? She told me to trust God like I have never trusted Him before. As she ministered to me, I stopped crying and from that time forward, began to hold onto Jesus. I decided to trust Him with all of my strength and with all my might for my healing. Little did I realize my battle had only just begun.

Early the next morning I went into surgery. There was no one there to encourage me or hold my hand or wish me well. I didn't have any family members there, and my three children had been taken to New Jersey to live with my sister.

My daughter, who was sixteen at the time, would take the Amtrak from New Jersey to come and visit me twice a month on Saturdays. It would literally break my heart into pieces when she had to leave. I knew it was hard for her to see me in that condition, but she insisted on coming, and I was always happy to see her. The boys couldn't come because they were too young to travel alone.

My children had to experience so much hurt and so much pain because I stayed in an unhealthy relationship too long. I wanted them to have both of their parents in their lives. Now they not only had one parent, but they were without either one.

I cannot begin to tell you the damage that may have caused in my children's lives, but I can tell you that prayers can make the impossible, possible. I prayed continuously for my children, and I still do. Even until today, I will continue to pray for them without ceasing. (I Thessalonians 5:17) I truly realize it is because of prayer my children are all living productive lives.

Chapter 4
Going Through the Pain

Psalm 119:50 "This is my comfort in my affliction: For Thy Word hath quickened me."

My sisters from the South had come to see me earlier, but they were afraid for me and were also afraid for themselves. They were afraid of my husband (who had been released from jail by this time), would try to harm them in some way. Their visit was short, but still I was so very glad they had come. I enjoyed every moment of my visit with them. Their love strengthened me and encouraged me to go through. I love them so much, and I knew they loved me. We have always been a close-knit family.

My co-workers were the best I have ever known. They came together to pay for my phone service and made sure I had television. Some of them would come and braid my hair. They made sure that I was taken care of. They even took up numerous offerings for my children and me. I will never forget the love they showed me during this difficult time in my life, and I could not write this book without expressing my appreciation toward each one of them individually.

The doctor had advised me that I would never be able to use one of my hands and would only have partial use of the other. I had to undergo surgery on both hands and endured many long hours of painful therapy, but thanks be unto God who always causes us to triumph in every situation in our lives.

God will always have someone there for you no matter what you may have to go through. God sent me an angel—a sweet German woman whose name was Ms. Greene. She was my therapist and someone whom I will never forget. God gave me favor with this beautiful angel, and her face will forever be in my memory. She encouraged me by telling me that I would be able to use my hands again. She told me the more I bend my hands and fingers and stretch the muscles in them, the more use I would have of them. She taught me how to be able to use my hands again through many tears and much pain. Sometimes she would even hug me and cry with me. She even had some of her patients to come in and encourage me to push forward and never give up. Because of her encouragement, inspiration, and the grace of God, I am now able to use both of my hands.

I still carry the scars, but I also carry the glory. Greater is He that is in me than he that is in the world or anything that satan can bring against me.

I share this story with you to remind you that as we travel this road of life, we will be confronted with many battles. The Word of God tells us in John 16:33, "In this world we shall have (guaranteed) tribulations; but to be of good cheer, for He has overcome the world." I want you to notice in this verse of scripture that Jesus said: "be of good cheer, for I have overcome the world." So even with the tribulations, we can still have peace knowing the battle has already been won.

In Psalm 35:19, The Word of God tells us that many are the afflictions of the righteousness, but the Lord delivers him out of them all. The Bibles makes it very clear that we will go through life facing affliction through our circumstances, but the Word also assures us that in spite of the afflictions the devil brings, there is total and one hundred percent deliverance out of every one of these trials. Our circumstances are just God's opportunity to show He is strong on our behalf.

Our circumstances (our trials and battles) are an opportunity for us to draw near to God, and for God to reveal Himself to us in a greater way than He has ever done before. God will use our circumstances to prove His faithfulness; He will use our circumstances to prove to us that He will never leave us or forsake us. Hebrews 13:5.

Sometimes God will allow us to go through difficult times, through hardships and trials. During these times He may seem so far away. During these times you may not even hear a word from Him. At these times we must always remember His promise to us in Psalm 23, "I will never leave you or forsake you." Everything God allows in our life is for a reason, even when we don't understand the reason. You simply must continue to trust Him with all of your heart.

Chapter 5
Letting Go of Those Things That Are Behind You

Philippians 3:13 "Brethren, I count not myself to have apprehended; but this one thing I do, forgetting those things which are behind, and reaching forth unto those things which are before."

You may leave God, but He will never leave you. You see, your circumstances (your trials and battles) will either push you away from God or they will draw you closer to Him.

I knew I loved God and I trusted Him. As life went on, I felt myself beginning to withdraw from God. As I was faced with the pain and difficulties of learning how to use my hands again, I became upset with God and wondered how He would allow something like this to happen to me. I began to think that I didn't want to serve a God who would allow me to be hurt like this. I felt so ugly and scarred and began to feel like God just didn't care about me or what happens to me. I stopped attending church and moved to another State where no one knew me. I just wanted a new beginning. How many of you know that you can't have a new beginning without Jesus?

As much as I tried, I could not let go of my past and found myself resenting all men for what one man had done to me. For years I didn't trust any man and was determined to never allow another man to get close to me. I hated my husband for what he had done to me; he had scarred me for life!

You see, I had to learn no sorrow will ever leave you where it finds you. It will either drive you from God or bring you near to Him. The remorse of Judas drove him from God, but the remorse of Peter transformed him into the "Rock."

I had to recognize that God's ultimate purpose is to do us good. Despite every negative circumstance satan brings into our life God wants us to be victorious. We must also remember God is in control of our circumstances. He will place a limit upon the circumstances satan can bring into our lives. These battles don't come into our life because God is angry with us, but these battles come as a normal part of life in a fallen world. God will allow them because He knows if we go through them, they will help us to grow and to mature. Sometimes during these battles, the dark clouds of mystery may seem to engulf us. We cannot understand why. A thousand demons may seem to surround us, making us feel there's no way out of our situation. Sometimes it may even seem that everything around us is dark, and God's face seems to be hidden from us. You may even ask yourself, "Has God deserted me?" I can truly tell you from experience the answer to that question is "NO!" On the other side of that dark cloud, the sun will shine again. You will look back on that experience and see the loving hand of God through it all.

If you are at a dark place in your life right now, take hold of the promise of God that He will never leave you or forsake you. Stand firm in your faith in God. Faith is just as much faith in the dark as it is in the light when everything is going alright. The sun will always arise in the morning, and the dark clouds will roll away. Weeping may endure for a night, but joy always comes in the morning. (Psalm 30:5)

This battle I faced was fought and won through the knowledge of God's Word. Gradually, I began to pick up my Bible again and bury myself in God's Word. One day as I was thinking about my past, the Lord began to speak to me from II Corinthians 5:17 – 19, which says, "If any man be in Christ, He is a new creature; old things are passed away, and all things are become new." He told me that He had given me the ministry of reconciliation.

I said, "Ok Lord, I love you, but I still hate my husband for what he has done to me." Please don't ever tell me to love my husband. The Lord spoke to my spirit as He began testing my love for Him. God said, "How can you say you love me, whom you haven't seen if you don't love him?" He began to deal with me concerning the "Love" factor.

As God revealed the real meaning of love to me and how much He loved me, I had to repent and ask God to forgive me. I asked God to show me how to love my husband—and He did. He took me to His Word in I John, the 4th chapter. You see, God commands us to love one another; for love is of God and everyone who loves, is born of God and knows God. But he that doesn't love, doesn't know God, for God is love. His Word tells us in I John 4:11, If God so loved us, than we ought to love one another.

In I John 4:20-21, He says in His Word, if a man says he loves God, and hates his brother, he is a liar; for he that does not love his brother whom he has seen, how can he love God whom he has not seen? In other words, God is saying there's no way it is possible to do so. V.21 and this commandment we have from Him, that if we love God, we must love our brother.

There was no doubt in my mind that I loved God. Therefore I knew I had to love my ex-husband. This was the will of God for my life. My desire above all else is to please Him; to be in His perfect will, not His permissive will. My desire is to have His perfect will to be done in my life.

Today, I can say I love my ex-husband, not for what he has done to me, but because the Lord showed me how I 'must' love him. I very seldom see him, but I no longer hate him. There is no hatred in my heart for anyone. I can also say if there is anything I can do for him within reason, I will do it.

I have a love in my heart for all people, because of the love of God that has been shed in my heart. I may not like the way people act, but I have learned how to love the person. God has taught me how to love people and to see the spirit behind the reason why people do what they do.

I realized in order for me to overcome this battle, I had to be renewed in the spirit of my mind by taking the Word of God and speaking it to myself. I pumped the Word of God inside of me until it became alive. Then I put it into action. I reminded myself constantly the God I serve lives inside of me. I made a conscious decision that I would rather die than to allow satan to steal what God had paid for me to have.

I began to see myself as God saw me. I refused to allow the devil to tell me I was insignificant or that God did not love me. I began to realize God had chosen me for a purpose. He began transforming my life into a powerhouse for Him, and placed me wherever He wanted to us me.

We all must begin to see ourselves as God sees us. He has chosen each one of us for a purpose. When we read about the great heroes of faith who subdued kingdoms and stopped the mouths of lions who escaped the edge of the sword and walked through the fire, we must come to the understanding that every one of these men and women had the same battles, the same failures, the same shortcomings, the same weaknesses, the same doubts and temptations in their lives as we do; but God used each of them mightily.

When we begin to look beyond our inabilities, our weaknesses, our shortcomings, etc., and see God's strength, God's ability and God's resurrection power operating in our life, we will be used just as Peter, Paul, James, John, and all of the other disciples, to show the world Jesus is not dead. When we grasp the revelation of who we are in Christ, we will become a vessel of power, working the word of God. However, we cannot go forward if we keep looking back!

Chapter 6
Having a Forgiving Spirit

Leviticus 19:18, says you shall not bear any grudges against the children of your people, but you shall love your neighbor as yourself.

As we flow in God's love, other people's lives are being blessed by us. That is why it's so important for each one of us to show love so we may express the image of Christ.

Instead of bearing a grudge, I realized I must bring this thing before God in confession and ask for deliverance. I also had to pray for my husband toward whom I had these negative feelings and if possible, take practical steps to resolve my differences. I had to find ways to show love because love will always cover all sins (faults.) Paraphrasing Proverbs 10:12, a grudge is something that does not get better when it is nourished. In Mark 11:25, Jesus called holding grudges against our fellowman "trespasses," which is very serious. It is a sin to hold grudges thus, we all need to forgive so that God our Father will forgive us of our sins. You must forgive in order for God to meet your needs. You must learn to forgive, no matter what someone has done to you. If you have a problem forgiving, just ask God to help you and He will. Just do what God tells you to do, and He will take care of the rest. After all, vengeance belongs to the Lord. (Deuteronomy 32:35)

When Jesus was nailed to the cross, He said "Father, forgive them because they do not understand what they are doing." Sometimes when people do us wrong, they don't really understand what they are doing. But regardless of whether they do or not, our responsibility is to forgive them.

Every believer has been dealt the measure of faith, and they can exercise it by feeding on the Word of God and applying that Word to their lives. This kind of faith comes from the heart, and not the head. The reason why people don't get answers to their prayers is because of unforgiveness. If your lifestyle is in line with God's Word, and your prayers are not being answered, the only area that is left is the areas of unforgiveness and love.

Holding grudges is similar to what happens when too much fat clogs the arteries of your heart. Fat collects around the edge of the artery and starts restricting the flow of blood until there is no flow of blood.

In the spiritual realm, unforgiveness builds up the same way. It will start collecting in the channel where the Spirit flows, and if you are not careful, it will clog the channel until no flow of the Spirit will come forth. I knew I could not allow myself to be cut off from the flow of God's presence by holding a grudge or unforgiveness.

There is only one place satan can attack you, and that is through your mind. This is where battles must be fought and won. Satan knows the only way he can gain access to your souls is through the gateway of your minds.

In the Garden of Eden, he approached Eve through her mind. Satan asked Eve a question which aroused her thinking in his direction instead of God's. Next, he went after her imagination, which is another function of the mind. He then captured her mind with the idea of being like God, Genesis 3:1-5.

Corinthians 10:5, tells us to cast down imaginations and every high thing that exalts itself against the knowledge of God, and bring into captivity every thought to the obedience of Christ. These thoughts are going to come, but the moment they do, you must cast them down. I had a Pastor who would often say "You can't stop a bird from flying over your head, but you can stop him from landing."

Your mind is not something over which you have no control. Each one of us has a free moral will. Through your mind you can choose to use your will in obedience to God or to obey satan. Adam and Eve chose to use their minds in disobedience to God, and thereby were separated from Him. The worst place you can be is to be cut off from the flow of God's presence.

Since I realized the real battlefield was in the area of my mind, my battle was to take full authority over the enemy and bring every thought entering my mind under control through Holy Spirit. I knew I had to root out, pull down and destroy all the works of satan in my mind. I had to stand up and resist the devil by casting out the enemy's strongholds in the power of Jesus Christ. Only then would I be able to have my mind fully renewed.

Romans 12:2, tells us not to be conformed to this world, but to be transformed by renewing our minds. Our thoughts must come in line with the Word of God. To be able to know the will of God and live your lives in obedience to His will, you must get rid of the worldly attitudes that have been programmed into your minds. You must come to a place in your walk with God where you will be able to say to Him,

"It's not my will Lord or what I want to do, but I want your will to be done in my life."

With God's help I forgave my ex-husband and informed my attorneys that I did not want to press charges or go to court. I requested that he get some psychological help because I felt like help was what he really needed. They were disappointed with my decision, but I would like to believe that God was pleased with me.

Chapter 7
The Weapon of Prayer

II Corinthians 10:14 lets us know that the weapons of our warfare are not carnal, but they are mighty through God to the pulling down the strongholds of the enemy. We don't fight our battles with the weapons of this world, but through the power of God, we can destroy arguments and every bit of pride that keeps us from truly knowing God.

Spiritual victories are won through prayer. Until you develop a spiritual relationship through prayer, you will not be able to lay the axe to the root of the tree and destroy the work of satan. You will be cutting off the branches, but never getting to the root where the problem really lies.

It will take preparation through prayer. If you are not prepared, you won't know what to do. In the heat of the battle is no place for you to start praying. You should have already prayed through and received an answer by spending quality time alone with God in your prayer closet. You must know before you get in the heat of the battle that the victory is already won or you will be defeated.

Nehemiah, Moses, David, Paul and other great people in the Bible, all had a spiritual relationship with God. This relationship sustained them through great travail in their prayer closets. This is the type of relationship that is rooted in total trust and confidence in God by spending time alone with Him.

These victories that changed the course of mankind were won because of a relationship with Almighty God. You must prepare yourself for these battles of life by going beyond the surface with intercession. You must travail in prayer in the Holy Spirit, and lay hold of these things at the root cause. The victory will come forth when you lay the axe to the root of the tree and not by just cutting off the branches.

In Luke 3:21 -22, the first account we have of Jesus, before He began His earthly ministry, was seeing how he used the two weapons of prayer and fasting to prepare Himself for the battle. At His baptism, as He came out of the waters of the Jordan River, He prayed. While His body was still wet from the water, He began to pray and commune with God. He surrendered Himself totally to the plan and purpose of God.

At the beginning of His ministry and throughout His life, prayer was always a strong and powerful force. Jesus had a vibrant relationship with God through prayer. He lived in constant communion with God. He would rise up early in the morning and go to a solitary place and pray. Before He would teach and minister to the people, He would always find a place where He could be alone with God.

It was during these times while Jesus was alone in prayer, He came to know God intimately. This is why He could say "as the Father knows me, I also know the Father. John 10:15. As Jesus prayed and talked to God, God made Himself known to Him in all His fullness. He revealed His character, His love, His mercy, and His power.

Although Jesus was the Son of God, His knowledge and relationship with God was not automatic. As Jesus was in the form of human flesh, it was necessary for Him to draw strength from God. It was necessary for Jesus to learn the things God wanted Him to say and do. In John 5:19-20, Jesus said He could do nothing of Himself, but only what He saw the Father do, for the Father loves the Son and shows Him all things that He does. Everything Jesus did, He did because of what the Father showed Him in prayer.

Just as it was necessary for Jesus to enter into a vital union with God through prayer, I know it is also necessary for you and me to enter into this union with the Father in prayer. You see, your knowledge of Jesus, your relationship, your union with Him through prayer, is the source and foundation of your strength. Unless you are willing to discipline your lives as Jesus did to include consistent times of prayer where you are alone with Him allowing Him to reveal Himself and His will to you, you will not be able to make it. You must be prepared and ready at all times to go into battle against the enemy and take the victory.

The seed of prayer was planted in my life as a young girl. Little did I know at the times when I would hear my Mother crying and calling out to the Lord in the very early hours of the morning that the seed of prayer was being planted in my spirit?

My sister and I shared a bedroom across from my Mother's room. I would often be awakened by her prayers as she cried out to the Lord. I would lay there in my bed feeling sad because I thought my Mom was sad. I just wanted to know how I could help her feel better. I did not understand until years later, that she was interceding in prayer. Those times of her praying early in the morning have never left my memory.

Later after I was born again and received the Holy Spirit, God began to bring my Mother's prayers back to me. I received what was called "religion" at the age of twelve because that was what was expected of you. The real meaning of salvation came when I was in my early 20's.

One day, a Mother of the church called me and said, "God said you were to be my prayer partner." (She would pray every morning around 4:30 am). I replied, "That is too early for me; I'm just having my second dream at that time of morning." She said all right but a few weeks later, she came back to me again, and I told her no and that she needed to find someone else. I told her I had to be to work by 8:30 am, and I would just be too tired. A few weeks later, she came back to me again for the third time. But this time I did not refuse thinking maybe the Lord really did tell her I was to be her prayer partner and I didn't want to disobey God.

This mother would call me every morning approximately 4:30 am, and we would pray for 30 minutes. Sometimes it extended longer, and I found myself looking forward to "early morning prayer" with her. That seed was planted over thirty years ago, and I'm still praying around that same time every morning. I Corinthians 3:6, tells us Apollos watered what Paul had planted, but it is God that gives the increase. My Mother had planted the seed of prayer, Mother Hart watered that seed, but it was God who gave the increase.

I continue to thank God for putting the desire in my heart to pray. Prayer has become so much a part of my life that I would feel lost without it. I realize the importance of building a relationship with the Father through prayer. It was through prayer that Jesus was able to penetrate into the realm of the Spirit and pull-down satan's strongholds on the earth. In order for us to pull down satan's strongholds, we must through prayer do the same.

In order for you to overcome these battles of life, you must pick up your weapon of prayer and use it first to come into this same powerful position in which you are one with Jesus. When you become one with Jesus, you are able to "see" and "hear" in the spirit what God wants you to do and say. There is only one way you are going to do this, and it is through prayer. The only way you are going to know Jesus Christ in all of His fullness is by spending time alone with Him in prayer.

In John 14:12-14, before Jesus ascended into heaven, He gathered the disciples together in the upper room to prepare them for battle. He knew He was going back to His Father in heaven and wanted them to be equipped and prepared to face the onslaught of the enemy; i.e., the trials, persecutions and the challenges of the world.

Part of the disciples' "battle plan" included the strategy of using the powerful Name of Jesus. Jesus told them not to be afraid, discouraged or depressed because He was leaving them. He told them they were going to do even greater work than He had done. He told them, "I am going to the Father, and whatever you ask Him in my Name, I will do it." You see these disciples weren't sent out to face the enemy on their own, and in their own names, but Jesus sent them out prepared to face the enemy, equipped for any problems they faced, with all heaven backing them up in Jesus Name!

There is no room in our life for defeat! Jesus was never defeated, and He has not planned for you and me to be defeated. The reason Paul could endure his many trials and tribulations, and not be defeated, was because he was able to say "I know whom I have believed." (II Timothy 1:2) Paul said "I am persuaded," and it doesn't make any difference whether I face shipwreck or whether I face all kinds of beatings and sufferings throughout my life," none of these things can be compared to what I know. I know there is a glory for me because it's inside of me. It is the manifestation of God Almighty, and nothing can be compared to that glory. We can go through every test, every trial, and every battle or circumstance and know we will not be defeated.

There is no room in our lives for defeat because there is a life within us that has never been defeated. Greater is He that is within each born-again child of God than anything that can come against us. The Father did not call us by His Spirit, cleanse us of our sins, and leave us on our own to live and serve Him as best as we could. God has placed His life and the very life of the Holy Spirit, the powerful, eternal Son of God within us. Just as Jesus lived His life on earth by the Father who sent Him, we must live our life by Christ, who now lives and dwells in us.

Just as your physical body cannot live without food and nourishment, neither can your Spirit live unless you feed it with the Word of God. You must learn how to draw life and nourishment from Jesus Christ and the Word of God. There must be a continual drawing of strength, a continual abiding in Him and His Word, and a continual communion with Him in prayer. It is through this union in Him that His life will be lived in you.

Jesus lived His life on earth by the Father who sent Him. In John 8:29, He said "the Father that sent 'Me' is with Me." The Father has not left 'Me' alone but the Father is in Me, and I am in Him. (John 10:38) Jesus was saying the words He spoke were not of Himself, but of the Father that dwelled in Him. Jesus' Words, His actions, and His works were all a result of the Father living in Him.

When you come into this union with Jesus where you are continually abiding in Him, and realize the fullness of the Godhead that is in you, you will be able to face and overcome every battle in your life. For Greater is He that lives inside of you, than anything that can come against you.

You must face these battles of life by knowing you are a son (daughter) of God. Satan does not want you to come into the full revelation of who you are in Jesus Christ, because he knows what will happen when you do.

Now is the time for you to rise up and take your rightful position as a true son (daughter) of the living God. It is in knowing you are a son (daughter) of God which gives you the strength and courage to face every circumstance or every fiery dart of the enemy without fear. Rest assured God has already given you the victory over poverty, sickness, and disease.

When you face situations and circumstances in which you just don't know what to do, do not lean to your own understanding do not try to work things out on your own. I recommend you pray. Know that the all-powerful, all-knowing Christ is in you to give you His wisdom and His guidance. Therefore, you can face your battles from the position of knowing that God has not planned any defeat for you.

One of the most important things we must remember is that spiritual victories are won in the prayer closet and these are the kind of prayers that move the heart of God. This is the kind of prayer that will pass defensive lines and create breakthroughs with God. But this can only come from you developing a personal relationship with God and spending time alone with Him in your prayer closet.

In the heat of the battle is not the time for you to start praying. You should have already prayed before you got there. You should be ready for battle, filled with the Holy Spirit, and filled with His power. You should know before you get in the heat of the battle that the victory is already won, God would have already revealed it to you while you were alone with Him in prayer.

Chapter 8
Dying to Self

John 4:34 "My meat is to do the will of Him that sent me, and to finish His work."

God purposely gave man a will. However, when you are born again, your life no longer belongs to you. When you are born again of the Spirit, your old man dies, and Jesus lives His life through you.

This does not mean all of your decisions will be made automatically or that you will not have any control over your actions or that you will no longer have a will. You will continue to make decisions involving right and wrong, but it means your will must be kept in line with the Word of God.

Your will must become Jesus' will, His desire must become your desire, and His purpose must become your purpose. This process is not optional, but this is a requirement if you are to live a victorious life and win these battles in life.

In order to overcome these battles of life, you must be willing to die to self. This is a continual process. You must be willing to crucify and put to death your selfish desires and the lust of the flesh daily. Jesus said in Luke 9:23, "if any man will come after me, he must deny himself, take up his cross daily and follow me."

Paul told Timothy, for if we be dead with Him, we shall also live with Him: If we suffer, we shall also reign with Him, but if we deny Him, He will also deny us." (II Timothy 2:11-12) You must be willing to give up all claims to your life. Every day you must be willing to deny yourself, take up your cross and follow Jesus by being obedient to God's will.

Throughout Jesus' entire life and ministry, He did not follow His own desires. He did not live to bring glory and honor to Himself, but He lived only to glorify God. The one driving force in your life must be to know and do God's will. You must not seek to promote yourself but live only to bring glory and honor to God. If you really want to know the power of His resurrection and the full demonstration of the power of God in your life, you must be willing to die to your way of doing things. When you are willing to suffer the misunderstandings, persecution, pain, discomfort, etc., that comes as a result of doing God's will; the power of God will be released in you to help you face every battle, every circumstance, every trial and every temptation in total victory.

So many times I have been cheated and lied on, hurt, faced different kinds of persecutions, mistreated, and rejected because I have been misunderstood. However, I endured and continued to show love. I knew by the Spirit of God that this was the will of God for my life.

If you are dissatisfied with where you are in the Lord right now, it's a sign you have not been doing enough. This is an indication that God is beginning a new work in you and through you with a new commitment. You need to cry out to God for Him to give you a spiritual breakthrough, for Him to touch your life in order that you may experience His power.

"The New Testament describes two types of power that God has given to us, "exousia" and "dunamis." It is the "exousia" power in Luke 10:19, which have been given to you to enable you to tread on serpent, scorpions and over all the power of the enemy. This means authority, jurisdiction, capability and absolute power!

In addition to using the power of authority, God has also given you "dunamis" power. Through the Holy Spirit, you have the "dunamis" Miracle Power in you. (Acts 1:8) This is the power Paul fervently prays that the Ephesian believers would have in Ephesian 1:9. "Dunamis" means miraculous power, ability, strength, and force. It also means inherent power or power possessed. Dunamis power means the divine enablement or ability to accomplish the work we have been given to do.

This is the power you and I need to accomplish the work here on the earth for God. Jesus gave His disciples dunamis power when He called them together and gave them power (miraculous power and divine enablement) and authority over the devil, and to curse diseases. (Luke 9:1) Jesus yearns for all of us to have this kind of power.

You must press on to tap into the full realization of who you are in Christ, and experience the indescribable depth of that kind of personal relationship if you are to overcome these battles you face in life. Overcoming these battles of life begin with knowing the truth of God's Word and being willing to die to yourself in your everyday life.

Paul in Philippians 3: 13-14, said brethren, "I count not myself to have apprehended: But this one thing I do, forgetting those things which are behind, and reaching forth unto those things which are before me, I press toward the mark for the prize of the high calling of God which is in Christ Jesus. You cannot go forward if you keep looking back. You must keep pressing forward in order to obtain the things God has already prepared for you. The call is to keep pressing your way through. "NO LOOKING BACK"!

Chapter 9
Casting Your Cares Upon Him

I Peter 5:7 "Casting all your care upon Him; for He cares for you."

Another battle you must overcome is worry. Satan's strategy is to overburden you with the cares of this world. In Luke 21:34-36, the Word of God tells us to take heed to yourselves, lest at any time your hearts be overcharged with surfeiting, and drunkenness, and the cares of this life, and so that day will come upon you unaware. V.35 "For as a snare shall it come on all them that dwell on the face of the whole earth. V.36 "watch you therefore, and pray always, that you may be accounted worthy to escape all these things that shall come to pass, and to stand before the Son of man."

Satan wants you to be so involved with the cares of this life, that the Word of God becomes ineffective and you lose sight of God's promises. He will cause your mind to be in a constant state of turmoil, overwhelmed by the day-to-day problems and trials you face. His goal is to weaken your faith. His strategy is to keep you so busy working that you are too exhausted to read the Word or pray. Satan wants to get you so involved with your own personal needs and your problems, that you won't be concerned with those around you who are lost or in need of someone to show them the way to Jesus Christ.

You must always take spiritual inventory of your lives to make sure you are not allowing the cares and worries of this life to choke the Word of God out of your heart. Worry is a common negative force that you must learn to overcome. Worry is faith in reverse. It will cause you to doubt and become fearful. It will hinder you from releasing your faith, and it can take control of your actions. Worry is like a disease that will destroy your faith, stunt your spiritual growth and distort your spiritual vision.

There was a time in my life when I would allow worry and anxiety to control my mind, making me doubt God's promises concerning my circumstances. I was allowing worry to control what I could see and feel which ruled my life, instead of walking by faith. Every time I felt I would not be able to meet an obligation, be late for an appointment or if I had to drive to an unfamiliar location, I would allow worrying and anxiety to overwhelm me to the point my blood pressure would go up. I would sometimes break out in a sweat. There were some times I would just become anxious without knowing the reason why.

When I realized that this spirit was not of the Lord, I made a commitment to live free from worry in the Name of Jesus. I knew the law of the Spirit of life in Christ Jesus had made me free from the law of sin and death, and I refused to receive this spirit.

I had to begin to speak the Word of God concerning this situation. I must admit things didn't change right away, but I kept speaking those things that were not as though they already were. I began to say Father God; I cast all my cares, all my anxieties, all my worries and concerns on you. I wasn't feeling the change right away, but I knew within my spirit as I continued to speak the Word and believe with my heart, these worries and anxieties would cease. You see, we have been given the power to cast down imaginations (reasoning) and every high thing that exalts itself against the knowledge of God and bring into captivity every thought to the obedience of Christ Jesus. (II Corinthians 10:5)

I had to take authority over the negative force of worry by first repenting for not trusting God in my circumstances. I then began to fill my mind and heart with the Word of God. When you begin to realize that Greater is He that is in you, than he that is in the world (I John 4:4), the negative forces of worry and anxiety will be defeated in every circumstance of your life. You will live victoriously!

You are God's delegated authority on this earth. God has told you to take dominion by the power of the Holy Spirit. God has given you the power to bound and loose through prayer and declaration. In order to overcome these battles, you must start declaring what God says about you and make that your daily confession.

As I have said, the victory didn't come overnight or over a few weeks, but as I continued to speak the Word of God over this situation, I began to see it turn around. These negative forces must obey the Word of God. God's Word will not return to Him void!

Philippians: 4:6-7, tells us to be careful for nothing; but in everything by prayer and supplication with thanksgiving to let our requests be known unto God. And the peace of God, which passes all understanding, shall keep our hearts and mind through Christ Jesus.

Worrying is like paying a debt you don't owe. I read that 99% of the time the things you worry about never happen. The Word of God tells us to cast all our cares upon Him, knowing that He cares for us and He will never allow us to fail or fall. His promise to us is with every temptation we face; He will always make a way of escape so we will be able to bear it. God has promised us the water shall not overflow us and the fire shall not burn us, neither shall the flame kindle upon us. (Isaiah 43:2)

To be fully equipped and prepared to overcome these battles of life, you must have on your boots with your feet shod with the preparation of the "Gospel of Peace." That is when you are not only invulnerable and unconquerable, but you are now ready to fearlessly and boldly march forward into battle, overcoming every obstacle . . . facing any kind of danger that confronts you.

Even during the fiercest battle when satan is attacking your body, your family, your finances, and your mind is under attack by fear, worry, anxiety, doubt, and unbelief, you will still remain strong and immovable. When your feet have been shod with the preparation of the gospel of peace, you are planted firmly, and you will not be moved.

Chapter 10
Maintaining Your Peace

John 14:27 "Peace I leave with you, my peace I give unto you: Not as the world gives, give I unto you. Let not your heart be troubled, neither let it be afraid."

The greatest battle you will face in these last days is the battle to maintain your peace (the peace of the Lord) that protects you from the worries of life. You must stop allowing yourself to be worried and disturbed. Peace is your security in the midst of trouble or turmoil. Your peace is a very valuable asset in your life, and you must fight to maintain it. Satan's objective is to rob you of your peace. Just as the soldiers picked up their boots and put them on to cover their feet; we must take up the preparation of the gospel of peace to cover our hearts and minds.

Isaiah 26:3 "Thou will keep him in perfect peace, whose mind is stayed on Him, because he trusted in Him. Perfect Peace means nothing missing and nothing broken. This choice is yours, but it will not come automatically. You must make the decision for yourself to clothe your heart and mind with God's peace. God's peace is a supernatural peace a peace which goes beyond our own understanding.

It is not God's will for you to walk floors at night worrying about your children. He has not planned for your mind to be in turmoil concerning your finances worrying about how the mortgage or rent will be paid worrying about how you are going to make the payment on your car worrying about how you are going to pay your bills or worrying about what will happen because you have lost your job. God does not want you to become anxious concerning sickness or disease that satan may use to attack your body. You must clothe your mind and heart with God's Peace. If you fail to do so, you will be weakened and unprepared to face satan's attacks.

Seeing that your peace was purchased with the precious blood of Jesus, you must lay everything that comes after your peace aside. It will enable you to be strong and strengthened in battle. Before Jesus ascended into heaven, He gathered His disciples together to prepare them for the battle they would soon face. The disciples were confused and afraid, and their hearts were filled with sorrow. Many of them were probably wondering how they would survive. Jesus knew their hearts and minds were in turmoil and that they needed something which would enable them to withstand the power of the enemy, so He gave them His peace.

John 16:33, "These things I have spoken unto you, that in 'Me' you might have peace. In this world you shall have tribulation: but be of good cheer; I have overcome the world." You must always remember that the gospel of peace which comes through Jesus, is your powerful weapon.

God has already destroyed the works of satan. When you are clothed in the peace of Jesus, you are unconquerable. It is a process that we all must go through in order to overcome these battles and receive the promises of God. But while you are going through you have the very presence of God keeping your mind in perfect peace. There will be nothing missing and nothing broken as long as you keep your mind stayed on Him and continue to trust Him.

You are in the kingdom of God. In His kingdom there is righteousness, peace, and joy in the Holy Ghost, and nothing in hell or in this earth can take that away from you unless you allow it to. God has planned for you to have His peace because of the ultimate price Jesus paid for you. Regardless of what you may face in life, maintain that peace at all cost. It belongs to you, but you are the one who must appropriate it in your life. You must reach out by faith and take the peace that Jesus offers you.

With your heart and mind clothed with His peace, you are guarded and protected from all of satan's attacks. Regardless of the battles you may face, you will remain immovable and unconquerable. Satan will try to steal your peace by bringing up sin in your past and try to bring you under condemnation so that you will not be free to serve God, but don't let him steal your peace. Remember the Word of God tells us in Romans 8:1, "there is therefore no condemnation to them which are in Christ Jesus, who walk not after the flesh, but after the Spirit."

When satan tries to torment your mind and try to make you feel discouraged and defeated, do not allow those thoughts to stay in your mind. You have been given the power and authority to cast down these imaginations and every high thing that exalts itself against the knowledge of God, and to bring every thought into captivity to the obedience of Christ. (2 Corinthians 10:5)

Jesus is not going to do what He has given us the power and authority to do, so you must stand firm against these battles that satan brings into your life. Let him know if it's a fight he wants, then it's a fight he is going to get, but when the dust settles, you and your God will still come out on top.

Satan knows he has no power over you, but you must let him know that you know he doesn't!

Chapter 11
Fighting the Fight of Faith

Hebrews 11:33-34, "Who through faith, subdued kingdoms, wrought righteousness, obtained promises, stopped the mouths of lions.

You must face these battles of life and defeat satan by taking up and carrying the shield of faith into battle.

Then will you be able to face all of your circumstances full of faith, knowing that God has already given you the victory in Jesus. All of the fiery darts of satan will not be able to touch you because you will be covered and protected by this mighty shield of faith.

When these battles of life seem to overwhelm you, you may think "if only I had a little more faith, I would be able to win these battles." Your victory over these battles is not dependent upon a faith you can somehow produce, but it is dependent upon Jesus Christ's faith that is in you. In Him you have access to the same conquering faith that enabled Jesus to confront satan and endure every trial, every temptation, and even death, knowing God would raise Him up, and He would come out victorious!

In order for you to win these battles, you must lay aside every weight and the sin of worry which does so easily try to beset you. You must continue to run with "patience" this race that is set before you. You can't choose the battles you will fight in this life because this is not a multiple choice test. You can't stop in the middle of the battle, and you can't turn back because there is nowhere to turn back to. You must continue to look unto Jesus knowing that He is the Author and He is the Finisher of your faith. (Hebrews 12: 1-2)

You must keep your eyes focused on the one who always finishes what He starts, being confident of this very thing, that He which has begun a good work in you, He will perform it until the day of Jesus Christ.

When satan attacks your body with sickness or pain, you will be able to lift up your shield of faith knowing satan has already been defeated, and that by the stripes Jesus took upon Himself for you, you are healed and delivered. By carrying this shield of faith, you will not only be invulnerable to satan's attacks on your life, but you will be able to move out into battle and even conquer areas in other lives.

God plans for you to have the same mighty conquering faith that the biblical "giants" of the faith had, and they were ordinary people just like you and me. Through faith they were made strong, and through faith, they became courageous and mighty in battle. By faith, Jesus defeated satan and raised triumph over him.

You must not look to man or manmade methods of producing faith, you must not even rely upon memorizing scriptures or positive thinking, but you must always look to Jesus for He is the Author and the Finisher of your faith. (Hebrews 12:2)

As you continue to exercise the faith that God has given you concerning His promises, He will strengthen your faith, and cause it to grow and develop until it is perfected and brought to full maturity. God has already planned for you to face all of your battles carrying the same mighty shield of faith that Jesus used to defeat satan.

God has given to each believer the gift of faith. Faith is a spiritual resource that comes from God. It is like a 6th sense. It goes beyond our natural sense of tasting, touching, hearing, seeing, and smelling. When we are born again, faith is imparted unto us. It is a gift of faith; it's God's faith. Because it is not our faith, it can come against sickness that tries to enter our bodies . . . This same faith will enable you to overcome every trial, every circumstance, and every problem, and make you more than a conqueror over every battle you face because it is not your faith.

You don't struggle to have faith and faith is not something you can work up. You cannot get faith by struggling for it any more than you can get love by struggling for it. Be mindful that man has nothing within himself unless he receives it from God.

Jesus tells us in John 15:5, "I am the Vine, you are the branches; if you abide in Me and I in you, the same will bring forth much fruit; for without Me, you can do nothing." The life comes from the Vine. That includes God's faith, and because it is God's faith that flows through us, it never changes. It never fluctuates, and it is always there.

The faith of God is extended in you and through you. Faith comes from the Vine (Jesus) through the branches (you). Your faith life is consistent because its God's Faith and God will never fail! It is a supernatural faith, and it is a conquering faith.

You can overcome these battles of life because whoever is born of God overcomes the things of this world! You have been given the right to overcome if you are born of God and believe that Jesus is the Son of God. You can use your faith which comes from God in every situation in your life.

People of faith cannot and will not be defeated! Yes, life is full of ups and downs, and we cannot change bad things from happening to us, but with faith, we can go through the battles and come through much stronger than we were before. Faith gives us that necessary inner resource to cope with every battle.

Faith is acting like God is telling the truth even if the situation does not currently reflect that truth. And the strength of your faith will depend on the amount of the Word that you feed into it because faith comes by hearing the Word of God.

Faith is a spiritual resource that comes from God. It goes beyond our five natural senses. It is given to us as a six sense (per say), which is required in order for us to operate in the spiritual realm. This six sense is faith.

Faith is imparted to us, it's a gift from God. Faith is not something we can work up, and it is not mind over matter. Our faith is always consistent because it is God's faith extended in us and through us. (Ephesians 2:8). "For by grace you are saved, through faith, and that is not of yourself, it is the gift of God."

Chapter 12
Prepared for Battle

I Thessalonians 5:8 "But let us who are of the day, be sober by putting on the breastplate of faith and love, and for a helmet, the hope of salvation."

Another piece of armor you must wear which will make you unconquerable during these battles of life is the helmet of salvation. This helmet is to be worn at all times. The helmet will protect and strengthen you against satan's attacks on your spirit. Satan's objective in all of his deception, temptations, and attack on your faith, is to cause you to turn your back on God. Satan will try to weaken you by causing you to doubt your salvation and lose the hope that is within you of eternal life.

When you know you have the ultimate victory over satan through Jesus who is in you, you are then able to fight valiantly regardless of the fiercest attack of the enemy. When you are wearing the hope of salvation as a helmet to protect your spirit, you can fearlessly and boldly hold your head up during battle because you will know your redemption draws near. (Luke 21:28)

The hope of salvation is not a natural hope, but it is a supernatural hope given to you by the Holy Spirit. It will assure you that God's plan and purpose for your victory has not changed.

Hebrews 4:12, tells us that the Word of God is quick and powerful and is sharper than any two-edged sword, piercing even to the dividing asunder of the soul and spirit, and the joints and marrow, and is a discerner of the thoughts and intent of the heart.

When you go out to battle, you must also take the sword of the spirit, which is the Word of God. The sword of the spirit, the "Rhema" Word spoken directly to you from God will become a powerful weapon in your mouth. With it will come the faith you need, and as you speak it out, it will destroy the enemy's strongholds. The Word is not only a powerful weapon God provides which makes you invulnerable to satan's attacks, but it makes it possible for you to conquer an enemy that has already been defeated.

Before you go into battle, you must study to get that written Word into your spirit and allow it to cut through and penetrate deep into your heart and expose any sin that is there. As you receive the Word and repent, the Spirit will cut and remove any sinful thoughts, the lust of the flesh and any hidden sins out of your heart. This will not allow the enemy to have anything he will be able to use against you.

Just as a soldier would never go out into battle unarmed without a sword or a gun, you must never face the enemy without first picking up the powerful Word of God, which is the ultimate authority upon this earth.

God's Word is Spirit, and it is Life to all of those who will put their trust in Him. Whenever you as a child of God speak forth God's Word, it is as if He is speaking it Himself. But you can't speak His Word if you don't know His Word.

The most powerful thing in the universe is the Word of God, and He will watch over His Word to make sure it will come to pass.

Isaiah 55:10 – 11 says, "Far as the rain comes down and the snow from heaven, and returns not, but waters the earth, and make it bring forth and bud, that it may give seed to the sower, and bread to the eater: So shall My Word be that goes forth out of My mouth, it shall not return void, but it shall accomplish that which I please, and it shall prosper in the thing where I sent it."

The whole world was framed by the spoken Word of God, and it is still standing. "The grass withers, the flower fades, but the Word of our God shall stand forever. (Isaiah 40:8)

Jesus did not once doubt when He spoke the Word because He knew God's Word would come to pass. When facing these battles, you cannot doubt and stand idly by with your hands folded waiting for God to do the work for you. You must confront and defeat satan through the power of speaking God's Word.

II Corinthians 10:3-5 it says, "For though we walk in the flesh, we do not war after the flesh: For the weapons of our warfare are not carnal, but mighty through God to the pulling down of strongholds." You cannot fight these battles with natural weapons, because you cannot fight spirits which you cannot see. Our weapons are mighty through God, casting down imaginations, and every high thing that exalts itself against the knowledge of God, bringing into captivity every thought to the obedience of Christ, by speaking the Word of God.

Chapter 13
Fighting For My Son

Psalms 23:4, "Yea, though I walk through the valley of the shadow of death, I will fear no evil, for thou art with me."

Approximately, one year after completing the therapy on my hand, my children and I moved to New Jersey to start a new life. It took some adjustment, but we were all grateful to be together again. After we had been in New Jersey for a couple of years, my youngest son wanted to go back to Maryland to visit his father. Against my better judgment, I decided to allow him to go for the summer with the promise his father would have him back before school started.

Two days before school started, he had not returned. When I called to find out what was going on, his father told me that he was not coming back. Again, it seemed as if my world was falling apart. After all, he had done to me I just couldn't understand how he could hurt me more by taking my son (my youngest child) away from me. I cried out and pleaded with him to not take my "baby," and his reply to me was, "He's mine too." He then hung up the phone.

I cried and cried hoping the hurt would go away, but it didn't. I couldn't eat, and I could not sleep. I called my sister for some advice, and she told me I should not have let him go. I told her I was only trying to do what was right and that I was going to get my son. She pleaded with me not to go to Maryland and told me that he might try to kill me for sure this time, but I knew I had to go.

I began to think back as a child how I had always missed having my father in my life. Even though my husband had tried to take my life, I still did not want to deprive my children of having their father in their lives if they choose to do so.

I was only trying to do what was right. I felt it was wrong to keep my son away from his father since he wanted to see him, so I had decided to let him go. I could not have imagined the outcome that would change all of our lives forever.

I knew even though I was afraid; I had to go and get my son. My oldest son pleaded with me not to go, saying his father was not going to let me take him. My daughter and I went to Maryland with the plan to ask for an early dismissal for him from school while his father was at work. We arrived at the school, identified ourselves and asked for an early dismissal for my son. The principal sent for him, but before he arrived at the office, his father showed up and began to make a scene. The principal sent my son back to class and told us she would not dismiss him until the end of the school day and we would have to leave. After school, my daughter and I went back to pick my son up, but his father showed up also. I feared being hurt again and returned to New Jersey and obtained a lawyer.

I fought for custody for over two years. Each time that I would take off from work and come to Maryland for the court hearing, his lawyer would conveniently be tied up on another case and would ask for a postponement. Finally, my attorney explained to me that my son was at the age where the judge would let him decide which parent he wanted to stay with and advised me to ask for shared custody. He explained to me that we would have to share custody. I didn't know God like I know Him now and I agreed. Although it was not what I wanted, I felt the circumstances were piled against me. My son's father in the meantime was giving him everything he wanted but not giving him what he really needed.

I cannot begin to explain the emptiness and hurt I went through by losing my son with only visitation rights at the early age of 10 years old. It left such a void in my life that I cannot begin to verbalize it properly. Every time I would see a child around my son's age, my heart would ache, and I would cry uncontrollably to the point of pulling the car over to the side of the road until I was able to get myself together.

I never saw it coming. I blamed myself over and over again for not filing for legal custody and preventing something like this from happening. I was young, inexperienced and not familiar with how cold and unfeeling this world could be.

My son would come to spend the summer with us (me, his sister and brother), and every other holiday, which was never enough. I would cry every time he had to leave. I felt like my world was crashing down around me without my son. Even though I knew the Lord, there were times when I felt like giving up this life, and I almost let go. God encouraged me through His Word and told me that the only way I would lose this battle I was facing, is if I give up. I then made up my mind that with God, I would overcome this battle!

My children meant the world to me, and it literally tore me apart for my son to be taken away from me. I was always with my children, and I always planned my schedule around my children. Maybe, I was too protective of them because there were very few people I would trust with them. They were not allowed to go to sleepovers and do some of the things I saw other parents letting their children do. I didn't care about what the other parents did, because I always wanted to know my children were safe.

A friend told me I was overprotective, and my children wouldn't know what to do if something happened to me. I only knew it was my responsibility to protect my children. I will forever thank and praise God for what He has done and what He keeps on doing in my life. God's grace undergirded me, and His mercy kept me during those years of being without my son. God gave me the strength to go through when it seemed like all my strength was gone.

Thank God we have a Savior that can be touched with the feelings of our infirmities. In every way I was being tempted, He has been tempted also. God knew every hurt, every pain, and every experience I was going through. He has proven Himself to be faithful to me. He never allowed me to be tempted above the things which I was able to bear. He kept His promise and with every temptation I faced, He was always there, making a way of escape. I was able to bear the hurts, the pain, the confusions, the misunderstanding, the doubts, the fears, etc. I am a living witness to the promises of God.

God is faithful, and He will do everything He said He would do and even more exceedingly, abundantly and above what we could ask or think. All we have to do is trust Him with all of our hearts and not try to figure out how He is going to work things out. We need to know without a doubt that He will work it out for our good and give us the victory.

I overcame this battle by the Word of God. I looked up every scripture I could find that told me who I was in Him, who I was through Him and what I have because of Him. As I began to meditate on the Word during the day and as I lay down to sleep, I felt a new surge of energy and strength coming over me. I cannot emphasize enough that in order to overcome these battles in life you must know the Word of God. You must read God's Word every day even if you don't understand it, read it anyway and the understanding will come. Your Spirit is like a computer which you store the Word of God into and at the time you need it, it will come forth. Even if you just read a scripture a day (or part of scripture), get that Word in your spirit because you will need it.

The Word of God tells us that weeping may endure for a night, but joy comes in the morning. (Psalms 30:5b) God turned my weeping into joy.

I moved back to Maryland and was reunited with my youngest son. We were all together as a family again and had an opportunity to see each other often. My son is grown now, but I see him often, and if I don't see him, he will call me every week. We also have the blessed opportunity to worship together on Sundays, including my wonderful daughter in love.

My oldest son is still very protective of me and is always there for me. One of my daughters lives in Pennsylvania, and the other one lives in New Jersey, but I hear from them often.

I never cease to tell them how much I love all of them and how much of a blessing they are to me. I give all of the glory to God for how He has turned things around in my life and is making them to work in my favor. That's the kind of God I serve, the one who will always cause you and me to triumph in every situation in life. Isaiah 54:17 tells us that no weapon formed against us shall prosper (He didn't promise that the weapon wouldn't be formed, but He said it would not prosper) and any tongue that shall rise against us in judgment thou shall condemn.

I would like to say to you, whenever you see someone praising and worshipping the Lord, don't judge them, because you never know what that person has gone through or may be going through. Every child of God has a God-given right to praise God. I have made up in my mind that no rock will ever have to cry out for me, Luke 19:40.

Chapter 14
A Lasting Encounter

As the years passed, I found myself again drawing closer to the Lord. I had built my life around serving Him and I was content with serving Him.

One day as I walked into the unisex shop where I would go to get my hair done, I noticed a new cosmetologist in the shop. When I walked through the door, he took a double look at me. I only took notice of him because he was new.

After finishing his last customer, he came over to me and asked my name. I was hesitant, but I gave him my name. He proceeded to ask me for my phone number, and I told him that I didn't give strangers my phone number. He then asked me how I got to know people and I replied, "I don't." He then told me to have a good evening and left. I was relieved for him to go and it didn't matter what he thought about me because I really didn't care.

Over the next year, I continued to go to the shop, and I would see him often. He was always kind and a perfect gentleman. I began to notice how he would always open the door for the females and how he was always helping them. At one time, he had even offered to carry my bags out for me. Slowly, I begin to realize that this man was different. He was not like the other guys I had encountered.

He was always polite but never tried to approach me again. One day as my sister and I were attending a New Year's Party, I saw him there, and my heart began to leap. He came over to wish us a Happy New Year, and we began a conversation which was the beginning of a long lasting relationship and that man became my husband.

I would like to say it has not always been smooth sailing, because at times it has been tough. We have had some ups and some downs, sometimes around and around, some arguments, some disagreements, and some serious misunderstandings, but with the grace of God we are still growing and increasing in the knowledge of God.

This man is my soul mate, and I know no one could ever fulfill me the way he does. I have uncovered myself before him, but he has never taken advantage of me. With patience, he is always there letting me know he understands, and we will work through these obstacles together. This man knows me like no one ever has and no one ever will. He is my best friend, and I can talk to him about anything. He is always there giving a listening ear. Sometimes I even wonder how someone can be so caring and patient. I sometimes ask myself is this man for real or am I just dreaming? If it is a dream, it's one that I never want to wake up from.

I'm not just saying these things because this man is my husband, but because it is true. I also realize at times it has been difficult for him to deal with the issues I had to overcome, but with loving kindness and patience, he has shown me the true meaning of love. I know without a doubt that God sent this man into my life to show me how a husband should really love his wife. I am truly blessed to have him as my husband. We have made a covenant with each other and with God, and a three-way covenant is not easily broken. We have not allowed ourselves to be ignorant of satan's devices and we refuse to allow him to bring division in our marriage. We understand what the Word of God means when it says, "When a house is divided against itself, it will not be able to stand."

We have not only made a commitment to each other but most of all we have made a commitment to God, and with His help and guidance we will be able to stand. By putting God first and following His principles for marriage, we have developed a godly relationship and are still learning and growing. I could not have asked for a better husband in reference to the love, patience, and concern he has shown toward me. There were obstacles in both of our lives that we both had to overcome, (and sometimes they still try to rise up), but because of the love we have for God and the love we have for each other, we are still moving forward.

I can truthfully say I thank God for bringing James into my life. He has taught me how to love and trust. Through the wisdom, knowledge, and understanding of God, he has shown me what a real marriage should be like. I have never experienced the love and respect that my husband has shown me. After almost 32 years of marriage I am still amazed at his strong but gentle demeanor and without him I know I would be lost.

I had a lot of battle scars both mental and physical, and I must admit I haven't always been the loving and understanding wife I should have been, but with the love that my husband has shown toward me and with God's help, I know this is another battle that has been won!

Chapter 15
Healing and Restoration

JEREMIAH 30:17 "But I will restore you to health and heal your wounds declares the Lord."

Healing and restoration came through the love, patience, and understanding of my husband, James.

There is a difference between being healed and being restored. Being healed is a process of being set free from trauma, grief, loss and pain, and the detrimental impact of man's words and actions over your life. It is being separated from all those things that negatively impacted your life. It is the breaking with all ties which violated who you were created to be; whether physical, emotional, verbal or psychological. It is the journey of being released from the grip of infirmity, abuse, trauma, rejection, tragedy and hurt in order to allow you to experience a life that is free from captivity, being released from bondage and into freedom from the power of lies and the influence of deception and God knows I have experienced it all. I wasn't living, only existing from day-to-day, but thank God for restoration!

Being restored is the process of being returned to the truth of your original identity and being able to walk out your journey according to your DNA. (Excerpt from 'A whisper in the Garden' by Sue O'Callaghan).

The adversity and affliction I suffered from domestic violence that impacted my life, could have turned me into a victim through the shame, guilt, and remorse, but it has launched me through a door to finding my divine purpose in life.

I thank God every day for sending my husband, James into my life to show me how to walk through and rise above all the manipulation, the judgment and emotions that had dictated and controlled my life for so long. With the help of the Holy Spirit, James showed me how to live in the freedom of God. I then made a decision to be a victor and not a victim.

I thank and praise God every day for sparing my life and how it has taught me to have love and compassion for others.

I also realize that there are still so many women who are experiencing domestic violence today and I pray that they will find enough courage to get help or even to recognize that they need help.

I realize that women have to be very careful when reaching out for help, especially if they are planning to leave. If their partner found out his abusive would get worse, as in my case it almost cost me my life. It is only by God's shield of protection around me that I am living to write this story; but God….

You must begin to seek God for direction and answers. He will lead you and guide you in the way you should go. If His answer for you is no or not now, be still and wait. Know that His grace is sufficient for you and He will give you the strength and protection to be able to hold on. After all, God holds your heart and your life in His hands.

God is showing His love for us through healing, restoration, and miracles. Whatever the enemy has tried to take away from you, God wants to restore it. Every day we have choices put before us. You can choose to continue to be hurt, wounded and depressed; you can complain and remain in the same condition, or you can trust God, and He will make a way to set you free.

The Bible tells us of a story of four men with leprosy who were outcast and didn't have anyone or anyplace to go. (2 Kings 7:3-4) "They said to each other, "why stay here until we die. And if we stay here, we will die. So let's go over to the camp of the Arameans and surrender. If they spare us, we live, if they kill us, then we die."

The men realizing their circumstances could not change unless they took a risk. So they decided to walk straight into the enemy's camp, only to find that no one was there because God has confused the enemy and caused them to flee! These men found themselves standing in the deserted camp of the enemy with plenty of food and provision all around them. These men had to set aside their fear which was keeping them and took a step of faith not knowing what lied ahead of them, and God took care of them. They set an example of faith for us to follow.

I'm not asking you to immediately come up with a plan today, but I am asking you to just start where you are with the resources that you have available, and see how God will help you as you go.

One of the first things that the enemy will try to steal from us is our joy because he wants us to be sad, sorrowful and oppressed. The joy of the Lord is our strength; if we don't have joy, we don't have any strength.

Don't stay in that valley of despair and depression. God doesn't want you to lose your joy. Don't allow people to control you when you can control your own destiny.

You may have been through some terrible times in your life, but God is the One who will bring you restoration. Isaiah 61:7 says, for your shame, you shall have double; and for your disgrace, you will rejoice in your inheritance.

God said He would restore to you the years that the locust hath eaten, the cankerworm, and the caterpillar, and the palmerworm. (Joel 2:25) Some of you have lost years to a bad marriage, but good things are in store for you. God is a Master of making wrong, right. He is still the Restorer! God wants you to have your dream fulfilled. He wants you to have joy. Don't let the devil keep on stealing from you. Start today declaring restoration over your life, and take what belongs to you, in the Name of Jesus!

Chapter 16
Knowing Your Weapons

II Corinthians 10:4 "For the weapons of our warfare are not carnal, but they are mighty through God to the pulling down of strong holds."

We must all realize that our circumstances cannot defeat us as long as we do not freeze, turn around or try to hide when we are out on the battlefield. Sometimes satan will use outside forces to bombard our minds with negative thoughts and render us powerless. When these hindrances come our way, we have a choice to make. We can allow SELF to control our action by yielding to self-pity, worry, and unbelief or we can cast these feelings down, yield to the Holy Spirit and take authority over them in the Name of Jesus.

When you are faced with these battles in life, you must recognize how powerful your tongue is and how vital your words are in determining whether you will be victorious or whether you will be defeated.

In James 3:4-5, James draws a parallel between the rudder of a ship and the tongue. Just as the rudder, which is very small, in comparison to the large ship that weighs thousands of pounds, controls the direction of the ship and keeps the ship on course regardless of the fierce winds and pounding waves, the tongue of a ship is capable of directing a person's life.

The important thing you should always remember is that you have a choice of being a victim or a victor. It is up to you to direct the "rudder" of your tongue so that when you go into these battles, you will know the victory is won through the words that you speak out of your mouth.

As you move out into the battlefield, you must know what your weapons are and how to use them. When I talk about picking up your weapons, I'm not just using a figure of speech. I'm not talking about some mystical object that cannot be obtained. Even though our weapons are not visible and cannot be felt with our five senses, they are still real. The two most powerful weapons we have available to us is prayer and the Word of God.

God has given us "spiritual armor" as defensive weapons to protect and shield us from the attacks of the enemy. Paul told the Ephesians to put on God's armor, which God supplies, which would make them invulnerable to the attacks of the enemy. God has also put in our hands offensive weapons to confront and take the power and authority over satan.

We are fighting and wrestling against unseen forces. Therefore it is impossible for us to fight our battles in the natural realm. Carnal weapons are not capable of locating these unseen forces that are at the root of the problem. The only weapons that are capable of doing this are those which God has created and provided for us to use.

One of the greatest warriors in the army of God was King David. As he went out into battle to face the enemy, he did not depend upon his own limited strength or any carnal, fleshly weapon. As he went out to face this giant who had defiled the God of Israel, he picked up his spiritual weapons.

David told Goliath, "You come to me with a sword, and with a spear, and with a shield; but I come to you in the Name of the Lord of hosts, the God of the armies of Israel whom you have defiled." (1 Samuel 17:45)

David was not fighting this battle with fleshly carnal weapons, but he stood clothed in the strength of Almighty God. His confidence was in God's strength, not his own. Even before going out to battle David told Saul, "The Lord that delivered me out of the paw of the lion, and out of the paw of the bear, will deliver me out of the hand of this Philistine. (1Samuel 17:37) David was speaking faith-filled words from the position of knowing God would deliver him. He had taken the time to build a personal relationship with God, and he knew that "Faith-filled words will dominate the law of death."

Your spiritual weapons of prayer, fasting, the Word of God, and the Name of Jesus may seem insignificant to the world, like the five smooth stones that David used, but they are capable of destroying every evil force that can come against you.

Prayer, fasting, worship and studying God's Word are all spiritual weapons which generates spiritual energy. When you pray in the Holy Spirit, you build up your faith and generate spiritual energy. As the Holy Spirit prays through you, you are strengthened and renewed in your inner man and your spiritual battery (per se) is recharged.

You must prepare yourself for battle. If you are not prepared, you won't know what to do. God prepared David (for great things) as a young boy of no reputation, the least of his family and despised by his own brother. God used the lowly tasks of a shepherd to train David in overcoming far greater enemies than the lions and the bears. Throughout his training by God, David gained experiences that would be the foundation of his faith in God.

Regardless of how insignificant your position is now, you must know God is preparing you for great victories in Him. You too must take time to build your own relationship with God, by spending time with Him in prayer and the reading of His Word.

Get to know His voice when He speaks to you. The more time you spend alone with God in prayer and in His Word, the more you will know His voice, and another voice you will not follow. His Word says "My sheep know my voice, and another voice they will not follow. (John 10:3) It's like a child knowing his mother's voice when she calls, or like a mother knowing her child's voice when he cries or calls out to her. They may be on the other side of the room, but you will recognize your child's voice from any other. This is the type of relationship you should want and desire to have with God.

David had the victory because he had a relationship with God. When it came time for him to go out in the battle to face Goliath, he refused Saul's carnal armor and chose the armor he was familiar with. When you are in a battle, you cannot look at your circumstance, but you must keep your eyes focused on God. To be effective in winning these battles you must be able to hear, discern and obey the voice of God. He will lead you by His Spirit and give you specific instructions on how to obtain the victory.

I cannot express how important it is for you to close yourself in with God in times of prayer and reading His Word. The time you spend alone with God will cause you to develop the ability to be able to recognize His voice. You cannot gain the victory unless you know God's voice and follow His instructions. It is so very important that you wait upon the Lord, being sensitive to His leading and move in His timing.

You must refuse to listen to the voice of self or follow your own understanding. Better yet, you should continue to acknowledge the Lord in all of your ways and let Him be the one who directs your path. (Proverbs 3:6)

Another important thing that you must learn in these battles is to be alert. You must constantly be watching and on guard for any attack of the enemy.

The Word of God in 1 Peter 5:8, tells us to be sober, be vigilant; because your adversary, the devil, as a roaring lion, is walking about, seeking whom he may devour. He seeks those he can seize and bring to destruction. You cannot allow satan to take you by surprise. Matthew 26:41, tells us to watch and pray. You should use prayer as an offensive weapon to prepare you for battle and always pray without ceasing. (1 Thessalonians 5:17) You must prepare yourself for battle by taking offensive action through prayer, against satan before you are thrust into the "heat" of the battle.

Let me remind you again that satan is our adversary the one who fights and opposes us. We are warned to set a watch and be alert of any signs of the enemy which may be lurking around. We must learn to recognize satan as a spirit, who usually works through people to oppose and attack us. We must expect it and prepare ourselves for it so we won't be ignorant of satan's devices.

You must not struggle and fight against people that the devil uses to attack and oppose you. Remember you don't war in the flesh but in the Spirit. The key to winning these battles we face is to know and act on the promises of God. People are not your enemy, so don't waste time fighting them. Rather, use your time and energy wisely and go after the real enemy.

Many Christians are defeated because they are depending on their own faith to fight their battles. The faith that makes you a conquering soldier is the faith of Jesus Christ that was given to you by God. Man, in his own human nature, is not capable of producing the faith necessary for overcoming these battles. The Word tells us to have faith in God. (Mark 11:22)

Your part is to speak the promise of God before you see the manifestation. Faith is a fact, but faith is an act. The key is the Word itself. Regardless of how distressing or how impossible your situation may seem, there is a Word from God to meet your need. There is not a problem in your life that a simple loyalty to God's Word cannot change; but in order to speak forth His Word, you must first know what the Word says.

It is so important for you to know the Word. Man shall not live by bread alone, but by every Word that proceeds out of the mouth of God. (Deuteronomy 8:3b; Matthew 4:4; Luke 4:4)

You must realize that your battles are spiritual, and you must destroy the enemy before he destroys you. In confronting these battles, God has given you methods and rules in His Word for winning the victory. You have to switch from fighting a defensive war to fighting an offensive war.

Jesus did not just sit back and take a defensive stand against the devil. He took an offensive one. The Word tells us in the book of Colossians 2:15, that Jesus "having spoiled principalities and power, He made a show of them openly, triumphing over them. God is telling all of us that we are not to take a defensive position either. "The best defense is a good offense."

Chapter 17
Strength and Power

Psalms 69:35 "O God, thou art terrible out of thy holy place: The God of Israel is he that giveth strength and power unto His people. Blessed be God."

Matthew 3:10, tells us the axe is laid to the root of the tree, but too many of us are spending time picking at the leaves and the branches, which is the outer appearance of our problems. We must lay the Holy Spirit, the Sword of the Spirit, which is the Word of God to the root of these spiritual problems of sin, lust, sickness habits, unsaved loved ones, etc., which are binding our spiritual lives. We have been given the power and authority to do so.

Luke 10:19 says, Behold, I give you power to tread on serpents and scorpions, and over all the power of the enemy: and nothing shall by any means hurt you. Jesus delegated His authority to us. We have the same tools and the same ability He had. Peter in the third chapter of Acts, recognized that he had been given the authority and he used it just as Jesus did. Peter spoke the Word when he encountered a cripple man who had been sitting at the gate of this temple day after day for many years. He said, "In the name of Jesus Christ of Nazareth rise up and walk" and the man leaping to his feet stood and walked. (Acts 3:6) This is the same power and authority that you and I have been given.

When you catch sight of the fact you are a person of authority just like Peter, you will begin to speak the Word with that same authority, knowing the invincible forces of

Almighty God are behind you. You not only have God's authority upon you, but you have His authority in you. He is acting in and through you with signs following.

The methods of the disciples were so powerful and so effective because they grasped these keys. They spoke the Word, and they acted in the power and authority of God Himself. Such a method can never fail. It works the works of God, and this is the same delegated authority given to you. It will always cause you to be victorious!

Jesus was determined regardless of the cost. He would not shrink or pull back at the thought or the pain and suffering He would endure. You too must be determined and set your face like a flint, knowing the Lord will help you and you will not be confounded or defeated.

God intends for you to be so full of the power and anointing of the Holy Spirit that even the demons will recognize you and will know that you mean business. He wants you to speak the Word with power and authority. God intends for you to rebuke the enemy, to tell him to stop and let him know he can't go any further. God has given you all that you need to rebuke and command satan and any evil spirits that are opposing you to leave in the Name of Jesus, and they have to obey you. Ask God to reveal to you by the power of the Holy Spirit, the spirits that are affecting the circumstances and problems you are facing right now in your life.

Once you have recognized the enemy, you must take offensive action. Move out into the battle from a position of knowing that Jesus has already destroyed the power of satan. Knowing Jesus is seated at the right hand of the Father in a position of all power and authority, and knowing you are seated with Him in that same powerful position.

The Word becomes a two-edged sword that the Spirit uses to expose satan's deceptions and even the sin in your life. Our hearts and minds are deceptive, and many times we cannot see the pockets of sin that are hidden away in our own hearts. (Jeremiah 17:9)

You must pick up the sword of the Spirit and allow the Holy Spirit to cut away all the sin and dead work in your life in order to be fully equipped for battle. Jesus confronted satan and defeated him by speaking the Word. The Words Jesus spoke out of His mouth were powerful lethal weapons hitting the mark and destroying satan's strongholds.

God has sent forth His Word, and His Word will not return to him void. He has planned for His Word to be in you and as you speak forth His Word, it will be a mighty weapon that will destroy the enemy out of your life.

Again, laying all else aside, when facing the battle of life, you must look to Jesus who is the Author and Finisher of your faith. (Hebrews 12:2) Your victory is not dependent upon a faith that you can somehow produce on your own. Jesus has placed His faith in you, and it is He who will cause your faith to increase. Your faith is dependent upon Christ's faith that is in you.

As you continue to exercise the faith that Jesus gave you concerning His promises, He will strengthen you and cause your faith to grow and develop until it is perfected and brought to full maturity. God has planned for you to face your battles with the same kind of faith that Jesus used to defeat satan.

Finally, these battles are not yours, they are the Lord's, and He will destroy anything that comes against you. Yes, God is going to fight these battles for you, but that doesn't mean that you should sit back and not face your battles. God is saying the real war is not to be fought with swords, shields, and spears, but with spiritual weapons. (II Chronicles 20:16-17)

King Jehoshaphat, the King of Judah, heard that the children of Moab and the children of Ammon were coming against Judah, and his first reaction was fear. His enemies were closing in around him, and he could not see a way out.

King Jehoshaphat declared a fast among the people, and the Word tells us that out of all the cities of Judah, the people (including the women and children) came to seek the Lord. Jehoshaphat prayed and acknowledged his dependence and trust in God. He told the Lord that they had no might against this great company that has come against them, and we don't know what to do: but our eyes are on you. (2 Chronicles 20:12) Jehoshaphat's battle was won before he went out onto the battlefield. God deliverance came because the people looked to God with their whole heart in fervent and effective prayer. The Lord spoke through Jahaziel, the prophet and said to King Jehoshaphat that he would go before him and that they would not even need to fight to win the battle.

After Jehoshaphat received the Word of the Lord, he began to worship and sing praises unto the Lord. The next day he appointed singers unto the Lord who went out before the army praising God and the beauty of holiness.

Prayer, fasting, hearing and believing the Word of God and praise, before the battle is won are the strategies God wants you to have in your life. The next time you face a battle, and there doesn't seem to be a way out, do not lean to your own understanding and be bound by fear. Put these same strategies into action, and you will not be defeated.

I again admonish you to spend some time alone with God in order to develop your relationship with Him, so when these battles of life rage fiercely around you, there will be such a knowing in your spirit that you will come out victorious!

The final and most powerful step of your battles is praise and worship unto the Lord, thanking Him for the victory, believing that He is even when it seems like He isn't. As we read II Chronicles 20: 22, when these nations came against the children of Israel, they began to sing and praise the Lord for the victory, and He set an ambush against their enemies, and they were smitten.

 Sometimes these battles are hard on your flesh. Sometimes the battle is more than a few weeks or a few years, but all of these things hinges and depends on the development of your faith. The next time you face a battle, and there does not seem to be a way out, do not lean to your own understanding and be bound by fear, but put these same strategies that the nation of Israel used into action, and you will not be defeated.

Your faith and your walk with God, at some point of time, will go through a season or point of being tested, but the trying of your faith is more precious than Gold. There is no cheating on this test. If you are going to graduate, you must walk by faith and establish yourself in this calling. You must take this test all by yourself. The test is the sixty minutes of every hour and the sixty seconds of every minute.

In order to get to the end of the battle, you can't quit. Remember the race is not given to the swift, or the battle to the strong but to those that won't give up. The only way we can lose in these battles we face in life is to give up.

How you finish is more important than how you begin. What really counts is being at the finish line when the battle is over; to still be standing at the end of the battle.

Let not him who girds on his armor, boast like him who takes it off. The one who lives to take the armor off is the true winner. The race is given to those who endure until the end.

You see, our victory is learning how to defeat an enemy that is already defeated! When the children of Israel begin to praise the Lord, their enemies turned on each other and completely destroyed each other. The Nation of Judah didn't lift a finger because their enemies destroyed themselves.

In John 1:33, Jesus said "These things I have spoken to you that in Me you might have peace. In this world you shall have tribulation (they are going to come): but be of good cheer; I have overcome the world." Yes, these battles will come, but you must remember that you are not fighting to get the victory; you are fighting to maintain what Jesus has already paid for you.

In Psalm 34:19, the Word lets us know many are the afflictions of the righteous: but the Lord delivered him out of them all. The Bible is very clear that we will go through this life facing afflictions through our circumstances, but the

Word of God assures us in spite of these afflictions, there is one hundred percent deliverance out of every one of them.

When you are going through these trials and battles, God will use these circumstances to reveal Himself to you in a greater way than He has ever done before. He will use these circumstances to show Himself strong on your behalf.

In order for you to overcome these battles in life, you must first take your position as an overcomer. This cannot be emphasized enough. In 1 John 5:5, the Word of God tells us that anyone who believes that Jesus is the Son of God is an overcomer. Eight times in the book of Revelation, Jesus orders us to be overcomers.

Overcome means to conquer; to prevail; to get the victory, to surmount; to overpower; to gain; to win. An overcomer does not retreat but will rise up on the offensive as he moves forward with his eyes always fastened on the goal. An overcomer may have some battle scars but will always come out stronger than he was when he went in.

I have personal battle scars from battles I've faced in life, but I am a witness that God is faithful and He has never left me or forsaken me. There is a knowing deep within my spirit that regardless of the circumstances I may face, God will always take care of me and He will always deliver me and He will do the same for you too.

Now do you want to continue to fight your own battles by winning one here and losing two there? Or do you want to follow God's formula and trust God as Judah did, and see the deliverance of the Lord?? THE CHOICE IS YOURS...............

ABOUT THE AUTHOR

Blondell Thomas Lives in Prince George's County, Maryland. She and her husband James were married for 32 years. They are the proud parents of four grown children.

She shares from firsthand experience how Christians can overcome the battles in life by applying the Word of God to their circumstances.

www.ingramcontent.com/pod-product-compliance
Lightning Source LLC
Chambersburg PA
CBHW052108070526
44584CB00017B/2391